# Unclenching

*poems by*

# Cindy Glovinsky

*Finishing Line Press*
Georgetown, Kentucky

# Unclenching

Copyright © 2023 by Cindy Glovinsky
ISBN 979-8-88838-345-2 First Edition
All rights reserved under International and Pan-American Copyright Conventions. No part of this book may be reproduced in any manner whatsoever without written permission from the publisher, except in the case of brief quotations embodied in critical articles and reviews.

## ACKNOWLEDGMENTS

Publisher: Leah Huete de Maines
Editor: Christen Kincaid
Cover Art: Cindy Glovinsky
Author Photo: Cindy Glovinsky
Cover Design: Elizabeth Maines McCleavy

Order online: www.finishinglinepress.com
also available on amazon.com

Author inquiries and mail orders:
Finishing Line Press
P. O. Box 1626
Georgetown, Kentucky 40324
U. S. A.

# Table of Contents

The Home Stretch .................................................................. 1

Gray Lace ............................................................................. 3

I Want to Be Bad ................................................................. 4

Stars and Ashes .................................................................... 5

I'm Getting a Cold ............................................................... 6

A Waiting Life ...................................................................... 7

At the Blood Bank ............................................................... 8

They Don't Know ............................................................... 10

Nodding off ......................................................................... 13

Office Day Jobbers .............................................................. 15

Holy Week at Work ............................................................ 16

Dr. Garn and Roberto ........................................................ 18

Four Days ............................................................................ 21

The Runners ....................................................................... 22

Grandtwins ......................................................................... 23

In High Summer ................................................................. 25

The Bully ............................................................................. 26

The Good Day .................................................................... 28

Day after Day ...................................................................... 29

At the PSC .......................................................................... 30

Cacophony .......................................................................... 33

Ten Years ............................................................................. 34

The Professional Student ................................................... 36

Power Walking in the Arboretum ..................................... 38

In the Fitness Room ........................................................... 39

Solitaire ............................................................................... 40

Powerless ............................................................................. 42

Encounter with a Great Poet ............................................. 45

Just in Case, Darling ................................................................46

Old Poet with Anthology ..........................................................48

Colorless ....................................................................................50

Walking Chelsea after the Sudden Death of a Friend ..................52

This Could Be It .......................................................................53

The Dark Doorway ...................................................................55

Look Up! ...................................................................................56

What Else Can Go Wrong? ......................................................58

Mindfulness ..............................................................................61

Starry Night ..............................................................................62

Swan Song .................................................................................63

Mourning Dove ........................................................................64

Sparrow Consciousness .............................................................65

Blossoms ...................................................................................67

Waterline ..................................................................................68

What? .......................................................................................69

Like Water, Like .......................................................................70

Unclenching .............................................................................71

*To all aging workers and retirees everywhere
and to my husband Ira, forever young*

# The Home Stretch

They gave me a choice:
I could stay part time
and retire a year from March
or go back to full time
and retire this November.
I opted for the latter course.

And then I thought about how,
back before our knees gave out,
we used to go to the track
behind the IM Building to jog
at six o'clock in the morning,
and how we would always sprint
the last half-mile.

About that sudden whoosh
of speed as, already winded, we
broke into the dash, with
one colored line after
another coming up under
our circling legs, then
slipping off behind and
how we puffed on
and on in the
black lanes,
just two more colored
lines to go now,
just one more, the
wide white belt of
finish line looming up
ahead, hearts going
like mad, throats
air-burned,
shifting,
finally, into
high gear
propelling

us forever
forward in

the home stretch.

# Gray Lace

What am I doing here    in this webinar with thirty-odd    sad-looking
overweight admins    sipping from plastic water bottles
staring at the Power Point    on the big screen
as the voice of the drone    from NIH    rattles off
the new terms and conditions    for 45 CFR part 75.210
in a monotone    something called    Uniform Guidance
whatever that is    I really don't need to be here
I'll be gone before I need to know any of this
after which no one will expect me to understand
this sort of bilge-water ever again
assume I'm too demented    I can hardly wait

But I don't know    maybe I just find it soothing
on a tedious February afternoon    with no op-eds
worth reading in the NYT    and only dirty snow piles
beyond the windowless walls    for an hour or so
to just follow the colorless office-speak curly-cues
winding their way through sections C.1.a and C.1.b
and sections E.3.a and E.3.d    in a disembodied voice
crocheting industrial-grade patterns
of gray lace

# I Want to Be Bad

Now that my days here are numbered,
can I finally be bad?

Not that I want to run naked
through some distinguished professor's seminar,
not yet anyway.

I'd just like to do things like
handwriting addresses on envelopes
instead of using the Envelopes function
in the Mailings menu in Word,
which doesn't work if the address has too many lines,
so it leaves the last line off,
and scanning through twenty-seven websites
to try to figure out what to do,
and feeling stupid because I'm pretty sure
I went through this before and found the answer
which is probably something ridiculously simple
that I'm sure you could tell me
and that I should have written down last time but didn't
and wondering if I have Alzheimer's
and calling the help desk and being sent on
to another help desk and another
and finally giving up after wasting half an hour
and handwriting the last line
on the damned envelope anyway
which looks worse
than if I'd handwritten
the whole thing.

Which is what I'm going to do from now on,
which may or may not escalate
into bigger, badder crimes,
in my numbered
last days.

# Stars and Ashes

Today is Ash Wednesday.
I went to the bank before work.
I brought a peanut butter sandwich
to eat at my desk tonight
and afterwards
will drive to the Episcopal Church
and put on my choir robe.
The priest will make a cross
of ashes on my forehead and say,
"Remember you are dust,
and to dust you shall return,"
and I will think that this is wrong,
that it's not dust but sea-water
though actually,
according to Neil deGrasse Tyson,
we are all made of stars—
stardust, the priest could say
to be more correct.

I will think this
but I won't say it aloud.
Instead, I will stand up
and go back to my place
in the choir loft
and drink some water
from a plastic bottle
and prepare to chant Psalm 51
with all the other
stardust choristers.

# I'm Getting a Cold

*(composed before COVID-19!)*

I'm getting a cold    poor me    which my husband
brought home from Boston    probably someone on the plane
so now at my desk    here in the office    at 2:33 PM
with three more hours still to go    I'm getting a cold

not feeling the least bit cold though    why do they keep calling it that?
even though everyone now knows    being cold doesn't give you a cold

It's not a terrible cold    yet    just the usual scratchy throat
and achy legs    maybe a slight fever    a real fever would mean
I'd have no choice but to stay home    in my favorite chair
with my white Denali blanket    with pictures of grizzly bears
watching one old episode after another of *Foyle's War* on Netflix
which is what I would be doing    if I were only retired now
instead of still sitting here    at my desk    at 2:34 PM    getting this stupid cold
that came from some woman in Boston    who probably got it
working in a daycare center    from one of the kids    who probably got it
from another kid    who probably got it    from his father    who got it
from an old man on a plane coming back from China
and now it's mine    poor me    to pass along    but to whom I don't know
. . .

Maybe you?

# A Waiting Life

A waiting life is not a life for all:
a hungry ghost that chews up nights and days,
diluting rainbows to a gray-white pall.

You pine for invitations to a ball.
An inward drumming fills your hollow days.
A waiting life is scarcely life at all!

While listening for that second shoe to fall,
you sadly miss the unexpected blaze,
diluting rainbows to a watery pall.

By now there's nothing solid you recall,
your past enshrouded in a looming haze.
A waiting life is barely there at all,

as one by one the hours creep, then stall.
Your chosen beast lurks nameless in the maze,
diluting rainbows to a vapory pall.

Existence beckons ghostly from the hall:
shadow of summer, winter, spring, or fall.
A waiting life was never there at all—
no rainbows—nothing, nothing but the pall.

## At the Blood Bank

My first job was in the donor room
at the hospital blood bank in 1970.
I sat at a desk and answered the phone
and tried not to mix up the lines
and gave the donors directions
and sometimes called them in,
which could be exciting
when someone needed AB negative.

In the back room
the blood dripped out of the donors' arms
into plastic bags wheeled up to the lab
on a stainless-steel cart,
and as each donor left,
I gave the person a slip of paper to take
to the cashier for $20.

They were called "professional donors,"
as if giving blood was some kind of career.

Some donors were students
and some were poor.
One man told me proudly
how when he was in Jackson Prison
he'd been awakened in the middle of the night
to go give blood for a four-year-old girl
who'd been in an accident
and needed B-negative.

On other days I worked upstairs,
in the office across from the lab
where we kept track of the units,
copying numbers onto pink and yellow cards
from the blood-spattered forms
the lab techs filled out
and where I wrote numbers on the cards
to be key-punched

so the patient could be charged for the blood,
which insurance didn't cover.
Most patients got only a few units,
but a few got more and more
and then, suddenly, none.
Every afternoon you looked
at a printout of patients' names.
After some names, was "DC" for discharged
And after others, "RC" for "respiration ceased."

If it was DC, you moved the person's
white account card
to another plastic box,
and if it was RC, you wrote the letters
on the card with the date,
feeling a little like God
as you filed it away.

## They Don't Know

They think
they know everything,
but the truth is,
they don't know
a blessed thing that matters.

They don't remember
the freedoms
we craved and gained
and the freedoms
we owned and lost.

They don't remember
only white male bosses
and gray-haired "girls."

They don't remember
how you mastered your whole job
the first week and after that
everything stayed the same.

They can't imagine
life without endless trainings
to keep up with the new versions.

They don't remember
how a computer took up a whole room
that only geniuses visited
and how you were hired
for your typing speed.

They don't remember
carbon paper and dittos
and stencils and little round eraser wheels
and typewriters that erased
when you hit a special back-space key
with an X on it

and typing the same page all over
because you'd missed a line.

They don't remember
keypunching and coding cards
to be keypunched
and taking whole boxes of old cards
home to your kids.

They don't remember
calling an office
and a real-live human answering
and if no one answered, too bad.

They don't remember
when office work was from nine to five
with a whole hour for lunch.
They've probably never even heard
of a coffee break.

They can't imagine
a world in which work was work
and home was home
and vacation was vacation
and a job was yours
for as long as you wanted it.

They don't remember
when you could schmooze
without it being "time theft"
and bitch without it being "whining."

They think there were always
building watch trainings
on what to do
if an active shooter shows up,
that there were always lockdowns
and campus alerts.

It makes me mad
how much they don't know
and how much they take for granted
and how good they are
at accepting the unacceptable,
and I wonder why we tried so hard
to change things
if this is where we were
going to end up.

But what I also know
that they may or may not know
is this:

Whatever
each of us inhabiting
this hierarchically ordered,
artificially lighted,
temperature controlled,
office space station
may know or not know

Somewhere,
beyond these windowless walls,
the sun still rises and sets
just the same.

# Nodding off

Editing a long, statistical paper
in the middle of a sentence
about environmental NGOs,
I suddenly find myself
on the back porch
of my childhood home
playing Sorry with my boss.
I yank myself back—
but a few sentences later
I'm in our garage suiting up
for a big ski competition
even though
I've never skied in my life.

I jerk awake.
My head droops
at a 90-degree angle
from my chest.
If I don't watch out, somebody's
going to come in here
and think I've had a stroke.

I can't help it:
My eyes pop open at 6 AM
but start falling shut after lunch.
They should put a cot in my office.
This is February, after all,
when all sorts of animals
are still hibernating,
Groundhog Day notwithstanding,
my last February behind this desk,
beneath this roof
beneath this sky
while somewhere
beyond these walls . . .
the sky is filling up
these woods

with snow . . .
whose woods
I think I know . . .
somewhere . . .

## Office Day Jobbers

How many of us are there?    falling into our days like dreams
scowling behind smile masks    cringing at buzzwords
kidding ourselves that our undernourished powers
can survive so much getting and spending unwasted
breakfasting on resentment    and guilt
at all the subversive little ways we find to feed our starving babies
musicians humming in headphones    novelists with hidden Word files
artists sketching in margins during meetings    dancers doing pliers in stairwells
actors learning lines in the john
and the mental health days we shamelessly take
and the extra-long lunch breaks    and the workstation naps
after the Muses kept us up past midnight

An office is no place for us    though we do have families
we should be out gathering material    working as farm hands or barmaids
not in this colorless, odorless place    where imagination can get you fired

What would happen if we all came out of our closets at once?
artists painting murals on gray-beige walls
dancers doing can-cans on conference tables
actors staging happenings    poets scrawling graffiti
a chorus in the atrium singing Beethoven's "Ode to Joy"
and everywhere the slogan: Art Lives!

They'd call security if we did that,
maybe even have us arrested,
but still . . .

## Holy Week at Work

This is holy week,
which I'm celebrating by listening with headphones
to the Fauré Requiem while proofreading a paper
on smoking rates in China

when my best friend Bonnie sends me an email
fuming about having to move to a different cubicle,
and I send her my poem about office bullies
and suggest that she quit DTE and join the Peace Corps

and the choir is up to the Kyrie as I read
that the smoking rates have gone down
because people in China really are smoking less,
and not just because of the changes in age structure

and Bonnie says she can't possibly join the Peace Corps
because she can't leave her sister who has lung cancer,
and I'm looking at the smoking paper references,
which will take me at least an hour to redo,

and now the baritone is bellowing
*libera me, libera me* from the grave
and I remember that this week is also Passover
and I want to listen, but just then

Rhonda comes fussing in
about some account sheet or other,
and I say some words to make her go away
and she does,

and then for a moment
I sit breathing and listening . . .

When I look back up at the screen
I see that the author has already fixed
all the references herself,
and there's another email from Bonnie

about the swamp cabbage and butterflies
she saw on her seven-mile hike,
and all the soprano souls
are floating up over the world
along with the butterflies,
like cigarette smoke
wafting all the way
from China.

## Dr. Garn and Roberto

The Center for Human Growth and Development
was on the tenth floor of the old St. Joe's,
where all the offices had been hospital rooms.
Every office had a window looking out
on the black stone Catholic church tower,
and you could hear the bells in the summer.
The windows all had screens on them,
and instead of air conditioning,
they set out big round fans in the hall,
and I wore a pink sun dress to work
and walked around barefoot in the afternoons.

In the mornings, I worked for Dr. Garn,
human biologist and National Academy scholar,
plump and white-haired and sixty.
Dr. Garn studied body types
and used things called calipers
to measure people's fatness
and wrote papers on obesity.
He had published over a thousand articles,
and we sent reprints of them
all over the world.

Dr. Garn hired me as his secretary
because I played the violin,
which he also played.
At my interview, he asked me
what concertos I'd worked on,
and when I mentioned Tchaikovsky,
he offered me the job.

Working for Dr. Garn was mostly listening
to his stories about people he knew
and how they were connected,
which in his world, everyone was.
He would start to dictate a letter
and a name would come up and he would say,

"He was on the statistics faculty at Stanford,
where he taught my student Arthur,
who married Judy, the secretary
who worked for Derrick, the nutritionist,"
and then he would be off telling stories
about Arthur or Judy or Derrick,
and it would take an hour to finish the letter,
but he didn't care.

Sometimes Dr. Garn would tell stories
about his childhood in Providence.
My favorite story was about the lady's maid
and the newly varnished toilet seat,
especially the punchline,
where Dr. Garn quoted the doctor
in the emergency room, who said,
"I have seen this sight many times,
but this is the first time
I have ever seen it
framed."

When Dr. Garn laughed,
it didn't make any sound.

In the afternoons,
I worked for Roberto,
who was from Peru.
He was a doctor too, of course,
but everyone called him Roberto.
He studied fish-oil and cholesterol
and things that happen
to people at high altitudes.
Roberto was short and dark,
with a sloping forehead
and slicked-back grey hair.
On my first day he warned me
that he talked with his hands
and might accidentally touch me,
and sometimes he did.

In Roberto's office was a closet
with cushions on the floor,
and every day after lunch
he would go in there and siesta.

He wrote all his papers
in a messy longhand,
which I learned to decipher.
Roberto was so grateful for my editing
that he listed me as a coauthor
on a paper in *Human Biology*.
I found this embarrassing,
but it got me a job as an editor,
with better status and pay.

I was glad, but after I left,
I was surprised at how I missed
Dr. Garn and Roberto.

# Four Days

On my four-day weekend
I finished the taxes
and watched three old episodes
of *Inspector Morse*
and had dinner at Zola's with Ira
and brunch at Zingerman's with Bonnie
and watched a pair of mourning doves
preening their feathers in the sun
and did four loads of laundry
and went to a meeting
and asked a woman in a bright green jacket
to be my sponsor
and dug through Rubbermaid tubs
and found the blue canvas notebooks
of the novel I started in my twenties
and sorted the papers into piles
and typed the first chapter into the computer
and read some aloud to my husband
who said it was the best thing I'd ever written,
though what does he know,
and the ideas came and came.

I couldn't sleep
and instead read Plotinus
and saw how everything in the universe—
the sun, the moon, the stars, the people, the animals—
oozes out of the One
like toothpaste out of a tube
and it was all delightful,
even the taxes,
on my four-day weekend.

## The Runners

Spring afternoons,
the runners are out in droves,
flowing along the sidewalks
in tiny shorts and tank tops,
some in ones or twos
and some packed together
in giant, same-sex multipedes
with legs circling in sync,
breathing mostly as one,
but with always one poor straggler
puffing a few yards behind
for whom I can't help feeling
a little sorry.

Each time another wriggling
mass of them moves towards me,
filling the sidewalk from edge to edge,
I stay my course as they divide
and flow around me
in two great rivers of bodies.

I pray they won't knock me down,
and when they don't, walk on,
wondering where they all came from
and where they might be going—
assuming they even
have a destination—
which they may not,
since perhaps their only goal
is to keep circling the world
or even escape it altogether
into some cosmic boy-
or girl-herd rushing,
forever young,
across the universe.

# Grandtwins

Doesn't anyone want to hear about my grandtwins?
Hey, you, look—here they are on my screensaver,
surrounded by puddles in a Grand Rapids parking lot,
Judy's arms circling Jimmy's shoulders
as though trying to protect him
from all the thunderstorms life can bring,
with a rainbow arching over them.
Isn't that just the sweetest thing you ever saw?

Let me show you this video of them running
across the Lake Michigan sand when they were toddlers
or maybe the one of Judy singing
"When I'm Sixty-four" when she was six
or the one of Jimmy break-dancing
on the living room couch.
And you've got to read the story Jimmy wrote
about the pirate ship that had a bowling alley in it
and hear about how he got the prize in Cub Scouts
for the most creative car, which he made to look
like a 747 jet—wasn't that original?

Of course, I wouldn't be so gauche as to brag
about all the merit badges Judy got in Girl Scouts
or how she's reading *The Lion, the Witch, and the Wardrobe*
and won the last soccer game single-handed
and has already racked up twenty miles
in her school mileage club.

What's that you say?
Your granddaughter did *thirty* miles and has read
*all* the Narnia books? How old is she?
Well, okay, she's nine and Judy's only almost eight,
that explains it and anyway,
I bet you don't have a grandson.
You do?
Ten years old and he's
already been accepted by MIT?

Yes, well, isn't that special?

(If there's anything I hate worse than a super-parent it's a silly, boastful super-grandparent.)

# In High Summer

In high summer,
there's still something left for me
after the eight hours,
and I march through the house
after dinner and make checklists
and clean out the broom closet
and toss old cans of floor wax
into a green garbage bag
and practice the song with the high A
and afterwards go for a walk
at eight o'clock in the evening
and try to see in the windows
of that house with the huge, spreading maple
and say hello to the neighbor's tortoise
and savor the white slice of moon
like a hole-punch scrap
in the powder-blue sky
and the phrases form and form
and I know now what the next scene
in my memoir will be
and hurry home to write
until the window turns black
and then write some more
knowing tomorrow I will feel very old
but not caring at all
in high summer.

## The Bully

My psychologist husband says Asperger's,
but he never met you,
so, what does he know?
Me, I'm more inclined to think
Obsessive Compulsive Personality Disorder
which translates to nitpicky arse-pain.
I worked for you nine years ago
for only about a year,
though to me it seemed longer.

My predecessor told me she quit because of you.
I heard that her predecessor was always in tears.
It took me a whole year to talk our boss
into hiring someone else to work for you,
but he finally did.

I'm sure you were as happy as I was,
and after that, we rarely even said hello.

Once at the Y, I glanced over at the Body Trec
and there you were, stomping away,
a skinny piece of gristle,
though I suppose you had to be tough
to make distinguished professor
in a field ruled by men.

I took care of myself, all right,
it's what you have to do with bullies,
but even now, nine years later,
I keep thinking up things to say to you
on my last day in this department.

The distinguished professor thing
might fool everyone else, I could say,
but it doesn't fool me.
Your accent gives you away.
I can imagine you down in some holler
battling brothers and a drunken daddy.

Did he lock you in a shed
when you were bad?

Was that why you sent me
all those emails with instructions
in big, block letters
and went ballistic
when I rented you a car
from a place that didn't give
Frequent Flyer points?

I'd love to go ask you that
on the day I retire,
but what good would it do?
I'm not faculty, after all,
as you so often reminded me.

If I were appointed God
the first thing I'd do
is give the world
some magic formula
to cure people like you,
after which you and I
might do lunch
and share our stories.

But since I'm not God
(or even faculty)
the best I can do
is write this poem,
which I know
you'll never read.

## The Good Day

Yesterday morning in the shower
I felt the bar of soap in my hand
and knew this was going to be a good day,
and it was.

Making breakfast,
I broke an orange apart
slice by slice,
and watched the egg's clear skirt
turn to white in the pan.

Walking, I cherished
a dance studio's purple awning
and a cardinal's whistle
and the smell of mulch
around baby trees.

At my desk
I glided through the hours
from eight to five
with world-class mindfulness
and handled each surprise
with finesse, even the darts.

In bed that night,
I promised myself I'd try
for another good day today,
but this morning, the soap
slid out of my hand.
I picked it up and told myself
today could still be good,
and it was, but alas,
not quite so good
as yesterday's
good day.

# Day after Day

Alice sips tea from a blue and gold cup.
From a half-open car window, a smiling Keisha waves.
A stranger calls about auto insurance.
Ira reads the sports.

From a half-open car window, a smiling Keisha waves.
Harry tells another joke.
Ira reads the sports.
Aunt Bessie knits some rows, then rips them out.

Harry tells another joke.
Mrs. Sellers complains of abdominal pains.
Aunt Bessie knits some rows, then rips them out.
"I'm really, really sorry," says Sam.

Mrs. Sellers complains of abdominal pains.
A man in torn clothes asks for spare change.
"I'm really, really sorry," says Sam.
Ricardo stands on the doorstep.

A man in torn clothes asks for spare change.
A stranger calls about auto insurance.
Ricardo stands on the doorstep.
Alice sips tea from a blue and gold cup.

## At the PSC

At the Population Studies Center,
on the second floor of a high-rise,
there were graphs posted in the hallways
showing birth rates and death rates,
from which I learned that the population
of the world was over five billion.
This was good for my sense of perspective,
since I was between marriages at the time.

Instead of being someone's secretary,
at the Center I was called "associate editor,"
and I had a self.
I had worked hard for this.
I edited professors' papers for journals
and figured out how to use Pagemaker
for our annual report
and conferred with Ron, the computer guy,
about some weekly handouts we produced
called "Techtips."

Each Techtip was printed
on a different color of paper.
The director loved the Techtips
and mentioned them numerous times
in the core grant proposal to NIH
to prove we were cutting edge.

One of the Techtips Ron wrote
was about a new invention
called the World Wide Web,
which I hoped would bring about
world peace.

Researchers traveled from the PSC
to China, Nigeria, Nepal, Russia,
Ukraine, and Thailand
and came home
and crunched some numbers

and wrote papers on fertility,
mortality, and migration
for me to edit
and then went back
to the countries with laptops
and taught their researchers to crunch numbers
so they could write more papers
on fertility, mortality, and migration
for me to edit.

For a while, I dated a professor who spent
half his time in Thailand
studying fertility rates.
He sent me postcards with pictures
of smiling, black-haired children
and when he came back
took me to a bluegrass festival,
and we made waffles
and watched an old Elizabeth Taylor movie
he'd recorded on his VCR.
By then I'd learned to play a little
bluegrass on my violin,
which I thought would impress him.
but it turned out the professor
only really liked Thai women,
and all he wanted was someone
to listen to his troubles.

Visiting scholars came to the Center
and the director brought them
into the publications office
where I took their pictures
for the annual report.
I liked the ones from former
Communist countries best,
because they always said my job
was important.

Once I got a letter from a woman in Alaska
asking if anyone at the PSC could tell her
where the best place was

to meet older single men.
She'd moved to Alaska
hoping to find someone there,
but said the men she met
were all either married or alcoholic.
I gave the letter to Bill,
who specialized in migration,
and he answered it
by writing an amusing article
for *American Demographics.*

I worked at the PSC for seven years,
then left to become a social worker,
having learned from the professor
who liked Thai women
that I was actually
a pretty good listener.

I was re-married by then, to a psychologist,
on whom I continued to use this skill.

Years later, after our health insurance
got too expensive,
I went back to work
for a professor I'd known at the PSC,
but by then the Center had moved
into a huge, famous institute,
and I was an administrative assistant,
not an associate editor,
someone else having taken that job,
which I wouldn't have known
how to do anymore anyhow,
and although the World Wide Web
had still not brought about world peace,
nothing else was the same.

# Cacophony

Now comes fall and the traffic is blocked off
while students in sweaty tank tops
carry cartons into dorms
and frat houses and firetraps,
piling themselves at all hours
onto front porches overflowing
with hilarity and battered couches
and bare-naked arms
brandishing beer bottles.

Walking to my car after work
past the bright green practice field
I notice a semi-circle of trumpeters at one end
and a line of trombones at the other,
jealous siblings blaring insults.

The Michigan Marching Band
must be holding sectionals.

Piccolos twitter down from the bleachers.
French horns gurgle into the cyclone fence.
Clarinets noodle and pace.
They are all honking at once,
snatches of "Hail to the Victors"
gloriously mixed.

Part of me wants to run from the noise,
while another part wants to stand and savor.

Instead, I walk on,
to where a snare drum fusillade
blasts the whole tootling mess to oblivion,
then subsides into a long decrescendo
as I step across the tracks
and into the chirr
of late summer insects.

## Ten Years

Washed up on waves of frustration
and unaffordable health insurance,
survivor of suicidal clients,
disgruntled students,
and book publicist harpies,
hauled ashore by an old friend
who needed an assistant,
at age fifty-seven
she came to this job expecting peace,
but peace it was not.

Instead, new troubles
swooped down on her like birds of prey:
week-long days,
colleagues who talked numbers
instead of feelings,
one heartless bully,
and a mysterious labyrinth
called M-Pathways
from whence documents
invariably bounced back.

For months, she grieved
behind her smile mask,
devising escape routes
back to doing "something real,"
until she decided, finally,
to make lemonade.

She joined groups, sat on committees,
found a soulmate, kept a journal,
and asked for what she wanted.
Then she put it all in a book
and the book got published,
and for a while she lived on dreams of Oprah
and royalties big enough
to buy her freedom

from travel expense reports
and a couple more years went by.

The book dreams died,
but by then she'd joined a choir
and was watching YouTubes
of her grandtwins every afternoon
and she helped her boss write a book
on American science
and life was good.

The days settled into an easy trek
and she told herself she'd found peace at last,
not by fleeing,
but by savoring the amusing email,
the completed checklist,
the honest conversation,
the view from the top
of the parking structure in autumn,
and those occasional moments
at four in the afternoon
when the sunbeams slanted down
through the skylight
onto her keyboard.

Finally, it was time
to say good-bye
and as she looked back
and saw those past ten years
flitting away like shy ghosts,
she felt proud of what
she had made of them

but, nevertheless, wistful
reflecting on

so many real things
she could have done
with those ten years.

# The Professional Student

My father
talked disparagingly
about people who waste their lives
hanging around university towns,
afraid to go out into "the real world."

But I don't know.
I think you could do worse
than pile up degrees
that won't get you a salary and benefits
in a town where too many others
have the same degrees
and, in between, do this and that
for the professors
who teach the students
who get the degrees.

I didn't get rich,
but I learned things:
like how to read Elizabethan handwriting
and analyze a fugue
and do a paradoxical intervention.
Not to mention how to key-punch
and boot up in DOS
and monitor a grant in Excel
and that I don't run the universe
and even geniuses
are headed for cemeteries.

So, Dad, when my turn comes,
if you're waiting with Mom
at the end of the tunnel
and want a report,
I'll tell you I spent
my whole life learning,
thank you very much,
after which, if you want,

we can spend eternity
discussing the merits
of my decision.

# Power Walking in the Arboretum

Twin feet go chugging, chugging
through tunnels of mixed greens. Blurred images

jounce frameless on either side.  Round rocks
in clay press up through rubber soles. A chickadee's

high-wire pitches tumble down and down
through latticed pines. This headstrong engine

pushes always forward, swinging arms like rods
between big wheels. Twin feet go chugging,

chugging through the lovely grasses,
long and soft, small gold flowers shudder

on their tangled vines, gray velvet shafts
of sunbeam slanting up ahead across the path.

# In the Fitness Room

Moving hams on the Body Trec lift and lift
To the labored breathing of rowing machines
Beyond the windows through three tall chimneys, souls of the dead fly up
Wisps of memories swirl away with the fine snow

To the labored breathing of rowing machines
A thin, sad clown steps and steps, a tattered issue of *Glamour* in one hand
Wisps of memories swirl away with the fine snow
On treadmills in a row, dreamers run for their lives without waking

A thin, sad clown steps and steps, a tattered issue of *Glamour* in one hand
The body builder, King of the Y, lounges next to the water cooler
On treadmills in a row, dreamers run for their lives without waking
Vacant eyes fix on the orange brick funeral home across the way

The body builder, king of the Y, lounges next to the water cooler
Moving hams on the Body Trec lift and lift
Vacant eyes fix on the orange brick funeral home across the way
Beyond the windows, through three tall chimneys, souls of the dead fly up

# Solitaire

In the beginning,
there was only one kind:
"Klondike" now,
"Regular Solitaire" to us back then.
My mother, who came from
a family of bridge sharks,
taught me to play it before I could read.

Later, she taught me "Bathroom Solitaire."
This one you could play sitting
"on the johnny," she explained,
with a little laugh.
I never tried that myself,
and neither did she,
but because all the cards
stayed in your hand,
we sometimes played it
on car trips.

My father's favorite was
"Idiot's Delight,"
which was easy to play
(though not easy to win).
My big brother David
laid out cards in pyramids,
then peeled them off in twos
adding up to thirteen:
four and nine, eight and five,
Jack and two.
My grandmother played
a simple game of fours
at the dining room table,
while devil's food
baked in the oven.

There was also a "clock solitaire,"
with cards laid out in a circle.

I think some babysitter
must have taught me that.

I learned them all,
then played them in order
from easiest to hardest,
laying out card designs
like patio bricks
on the back porch table
or on a big wooden tray
during the Asian flu.

Solitaire then
was a job to be done,
and worth doing well.

Now, in old age,
I've forgotten all those games—
all but Klondike,
which I play every night
on the computer,
three rounds only.
I don't much care if I win.
I don't care either to learn
every kind of solitaire there is
and bore everybody
bragging about my latest "passion"
and enter some competition
for world-champion
solitairist.

I just like the way it feels
when card after card is the one I need,
and everything falls into place.

# Powerless

Can't meet, can't print, can't cook.
Can't vacuum, can't watch, can't see.
Can't, can't, can't . . .

Why did I marry him?
A million reasons, actually,
but his whining at times like this
wasn't one of them.

"Give it a break, dear," I'll say
when he starts in again.
"Summer storms happen.
This can't last forever.
I think I saw a crew up the street
fiddling with that box on the corner.
That's a good sign, isn't it?"

We should have gotten the grill fixed.
We should have bought more batteries.
We should have bought a generator.
Should, should, should . . .

"So, what's the matter?" I could say.
"Have you never been powerless before?
Is this a new experience for you?
Well, think of that!
I've been powerless my whole life
about all sorts of things,
which is maybe why
I'm so much better at this
than you are"—
that's what I'd like to say,
though I won't.

But really, he doesn't know what it's like:
That God-awful thing every month from 14 to 50,
then hot flashes and mood swings,

not to mention the baby ordeal.
And, meanwhile,
a lot of type A white humanoids
with big shoulders—
and that silly, dangling would-be
weapon between their legs—
trashing our life decisions.

Which all the Power Suits, Power Walking,
Power Stances, Empowerment, Higher Power
in the world will never
entirely prevent, I'm convinced.

I've learned to do what I can,
even if it's not much.

Which is why,
when the lights went out:
*I* called the electric company,
unplugged the computers, lit the candles,
found the flashlights, phoned the restaurants,
turned on the radio, bought the batteries,
and tossed the rotting meat,
while *he* sat in his chair and stewed:

About the work he couldn't do,
And the mess in the house,
And the aches in his joints,
And the state of the world.

But of course—
Since coping is what I do,
I can cope with that too!
Reframe his kvetching as static
on some cheap transistor,
and tell myself it's the price I pay
for the good times.

Just one more thing over which,
until death do us part,
I remain eternally,
resignedly

POWERLESS!

# Encounter with a Great Poet

On Sunday night I woke up feeling sick.
Waiting to vomit, I read through a book
of Billy Collins. Finally, I went back to sleep.

I dreamed the poet and I sat in two rocking chairs.
I asked him how he wrote his poems,
and he said that was something one didn't ask.

Then he was in bed next to me.
I was excited to be next to a Great Poet
until I remembered I was supposed to call you.

I got up and went out with my phone.
The hallways were painted a hideous turquoise.
I had forgotten the number of our room.

I was still wandering when you got up
to go down to the treadmill, while the poet,
behind the door with the blurred number,
lay wondering what had become of me.

# Just in Case, Darling

Will there really ever come a day:
when you don't believe you have cancer of the esophagus
and I don't have a suspicious-looking age spot
and we have enough in the bank to pay every bill in the basket
and your daughter isn't dating a loser,
and my son hasn't quit his job to run for Congress,
and the cat hasn't come staggering home with tooth-marks on his shoulder
and the dog isn't licking his privates for hours on end
and all the computers work
and all the printers work
and all the cell phones work
and nobody's car is making a noise like rocks in a blender
and nobody's tooth just lost a cusp
and all the flags are flying at the tops of their masts
and all our neighbors are nice
and all our shoes fit
and all our toilets flush
without running?

Will there ever come a day
when all our troubles just stop,
like broken clocks,
and leave us with nothing to do
but stare out across our brown back fence,
with minds as quiet as lakes?

A day like that may be worth
waiting a lifetime for—
I'm not saying it's not—
But just in case it never arrives, darling,
won't you please
come sit beside me now
exactly as we are
and examine the tiny
shells in this shoebox
one by one

and taste the scent
of crumbling yellow leaves
in the warm air?

# Old Poet with Anthology

She turned the page,
and the poem took her back
to cantering horses and Iowa cornfields.

Read another that was a riddle
and felt clever when she figured out
that the "I" in the poem was sand.

There was a poem that rhymed,
which she whispered aloud to herself,
tapping the rocking chair arm.

A poem that made her visualize
an old red barrow from her childhood
and reach for its two handles.

An opaque poem that defeated her,
though she also wondered if the emperor
really had clothes on.

A poem that hugged her close,
and told her a fellow pilgrim's sorrow
matched her sorrow.

One poem made her
put the book down and invoke Google
on gods and goddesses.

Another carried her
along an ancient river of vowels
through a waking dream.

There was a poem that placed her inside
an Other, defined by
color, shape, and ancestors.

A purplish poem that
made her wonder what the editor
could have been thinking.

A poem that taught her to see
our ordinary moon
as a brand-new moon.

And a poem about a cross
that looked like a cross,
which she admired but did not like.

A poem that transported her
to a South Sea refuge
of orange and green birds.

A poem built from a jungle
of surprising word combinations
that gave her a headache.

A poem so gruesome
she stopped reading and wondered
what the world was coming to.

A poem that made her chuckle,
a poem that made her weep,
a poem that drained the blood from her veins.

And, finally, the poem that made her
want to quit writing poems
because the poet had already said
everything she wanted to say,
and because she knew
she could never ever hope
to write anything—
anything at all—
that came even close
to being
that beautiful.

## Colorless

Born in the directionless middle,
raised on beefsteak and normalcy,
with nothing-colored hair,
nothing-colored eyes,
nothing-colored skin,
pale, chinless face,
and uninflected voice,
what could I possibly have to say
in this Iowa monotone
that the colorful and the bruised
would want to hear?

What magic words might enable
this aging outline of a human being,
struggling to remember
the latest words
we're not supposed to use,
to connect?

I have no orange and green memories
of failed countries to describe,
no snippets of jazz tunes
or stories of lynchings by monsters
whose pale skins
bequeathed me their guilt.
I can't talk about being beaten
for loving the one I love
or raped by a drunken daddy.
I've never been homeless
(though I've sometimes been afraid).
I can try to sympathize, but really,
I haven't a clue.

Nothing I say will ring true,
so why say anything at all?

Better to go stand under a tree
and feel all the terrible, beautiful
colors of the world pass through
my jellyfish membranes
like planes through O'Hare.

Better to hold my peace,
and count my breaths,
and reinvent my colorless self
as transparent eyeball.

# Walking Chelsea after the Sudden Death of a Friend

*for Liz*

Oh, please, let me keep
even this soggy world,
snow puddles and all.

Let me keep that shred of colorless
plastic fluttering from branches
like iv poles beyond the back fence.

Those pine tops marking places
between blackened condo walls—
let me keep those too.

And, of course, keep
my darling blond cocker Chelsea rooting
through snow piles for fresh dog doo cigars,
Chelsea I *must* keep!

Keep those myriad ghost veins
etched white in asphalt
sprinkled with salt crystals.
Keep this everyday skirt
spread out in drizzled folds—
browns grays blacks whites—
Michigan winter shades.
Keep even the grimy, blood-red
SUV blocking the view.

Just let me keep,
for a little longer anyway,
what one good woman
no longer
has.

# This Could Be It

Because,
after the bloodwork comes back,
you just know this is It,
even though you still feel fine
and the doctor hasn't actually
told you that,

You begin making plans
to buy a big-screen TV for the bedroom
and show your spouse how to access Fidelity
and visit the Berkshires one last time.

You rehearse telling your loved ones the bad news
and start mentally drafting your obituary,
knowing that if you leave it up to them,
they'll leave out all the best stuff.

You reread Donald Hall's poem
about Jane Kenyon dying of leukemia
and pull out that book on pain management
you've been meaning to read.

You think about how, notwithstanding prediabetes,
when your doctor finally gives you the word,
you'll go to Ben and Jerry's and get yourself
the biggest hot fudge sundae on the menu.

You go for a walk to look at the leaves
and stand staring at one
gorgeous red tree for a long time,
just knowing that this may be
the last gorgeous red tree
you'll ever get to see.

But then . . .

You Google and discover
that the African lymphoma
that killed your dad at age seventy
isn't hereditary,
and your doctor calls
to tell you this isn't It,
not yet anyhow,
sending you back to Plan A,
back from funeral fantasies
to decluttering and checkbooks
and Thanksgiving dinner
in less than a month.

And meanwhile,
it strikes you that the red leaves
aren't quite so gorgeous now as they were
when you just knew this was It
and you're forced to admit
that although you're relieved,
yes, you certainly are,
no doubt about that,

You can't help missing
believing this was It
just a little.

# The Dark Doorway

Not a door, but a doorway.
You could march right up into it—
the solid rectangle of black infinity
next to the flung-back slab in the wall
of some Yorkshire outbuilding, perhaps.

My stepdaughter's Christmas gift—
found in the trash, she told her dad—
the black-and-white photo,
artist unknown,
hangs at the top of our stairs.

Most of the time I pass right by it
without pausing to look,
though I can feel its refusal
pressing into my back as I turn.

It's just a picture, I tell myself.
It doesn't belong here, really.
The only dark thing
in this houseful of color.
Why don't we put it on E-bay?

But maybe it's like one of those Zen koans
leading from everything to nothing.
Like Ash Wednesday
or black nightgowns
or something in Sartre.

A thing to stare down into
as a form of exercise,
barbells for the soul.
Into and also through—
on the off chance
that back in the dark shed,
some stray hand might be
fumbling for a switch
to flood the doorway
with light.

# Look Up!

>   *Inspired by Bill Allen's sculpture "Burial Ground,"*
>   *Dennos Museum, Traverse City, Michigan*

Black mummy bound,
mouths dirt-gagged,
straight-jacketed armless
by flesh-keeping peat;

We cannot speak
    cannot gesture
    cannot dance
    cannot hug;

We can only speak with our eyes,
our collective, magnetic eyes,
the collective eyes of the enslaved;

We can only stand tall,
cast collective eyes upward
in one long silent gospel chorus
      of pleading
      of calling
      of beckoning,
raising our silent eyes
in a monumental roar
until, amazingly,

White splotches blossom out above us!
Stars of Bethlehem descending,
Gabriel blowing his horn
as we stand here together,
awestruck and unafraid:

The Lord's sweet chariots swinging down
to carry us all up yonder,
up to where our dirt-plugged voices
are free at last to sing:

Hallelujah!
Hallelujah!

Look up!

# What Else Can Go Wrong?

> *I'm an old man and have known a great many troubles,
> most of which never happened.*
> Mark Twain

As usual, the worries are lined up
like schoolkids, single file,
pushing to get through the door.

So, my blood work came back normal,
and maybe I'm not going to die of lymphoma
like my dad did at age seventy,
what's next?

I just know the condo manager,
who never does what he says he's going to do,
won't really have the water shut off
at 8:30 tomorrow like he promised
and the plumber will come here for nothing
and be mad at me, not the manager,
and charge us a huge bill
that the management company should pay
but, of course, won't.

And when the water does get shut off
and the plumber doesn't get mad,
and I don't lose my temper
and behave like a two-year-old,
I still won't have heard back
from Dorothy at Stillwater Books,
whom I emailed three times
asking for the link I need
to do my virtual reading next Thursday
which all my best Facebook friends
have promised to attend.

And after I get Dorothy's email with the link,
I can worry about a blowout on the highway

from the huge pothole I drove over
taking old clothes to the Salvation Army
and the trip to the hospital in the ambulance
with all my bones broken
and the police at the door
giving Ira the bad news.

And if I do, by some miracle,
make it to the bookstore in Marshall alive,
it will only be to sit at a table
worrying about my book being a bust,
and my character defects
and my wasted life
while all the customers
ignore me.

And when I get home safe and sound
and the bathroom is all finished
and I don't have lymphoma
and a couple of people
even bought my book,
I can look at the weather forecast
and worry about the storm predicted
on Tuesday afternoon, which is sure
to knock the power out again,
or maybe even knock
our house down this time.

And when on Tuesday
the red patches on the radar map
part like the Red Sea
and move harmlessly past our town,
I'll need to find something else
to worry over.

Because, without my perpetual worrying,
who knows what catastrophes
might have occurred?
Yes, I know,

I could give it a break,
as others have advised,
do some reframing,
say some affirmations,
but would I really want to risk that?

I just know that
the moment my back is turned,
and I'm dancing a worry-free waltz,
focusing on my breathing
and living in the moment,
right here, right now,
the doctor will call with bad news,
or the roof will cave in,
or World War III will begin.

But don't worry:
none of those things is going to happen.
I'm not going to let them.
No, siree!
I'll stand fast,
holding them at bay
with a steady onslaught of worries,
knowing there's always
something new I can worry about,
if only the toxic effects
of all this worrying.

# Mindfulness

This is one of those days
when the mind sits on the moment
like a hat on a head,
A hat with eyes that see and see:
The brown squirrel scratching itself;
The ash-filled fireplace;
Shovelfuls disappearing one by one
into a brown paper bag;
The bag held by a hand
looking suddenly so strange
one can't help wondering
what a Martian would think of it;
The bowl of steel cut oats;
The yellow flash of an idea
from God knows where;
The long spiral of black lace
newspaper sentences;
And, meanwhile, the mind itself
nimbly detoxifying
every cloud of sorrow, anger, or fear
that passes across
the inner dark.

## Starry Night

Like Freud, it's hard to stomach for too long.
Your eyes skitter frameward
fleeing finger-painted yellow whorls
that suck them back mid-rectangle
to tumble like broken shells
beneath the spiral-wave on the right.

Better to pull away—
come into a room with powder blue walls,
table, chairs, pitcher, brush, and bedstead,
or wake up lying in the hay at noon,
with barefoot peasants, shoes and scythes.

Anywhere but here,
trapped in a mind
cut loose from its moorings,
a few black finger strokes
of rooftops and steeple
in one corner.

It's hard to say which is more disturbing:
The yellow gullet swallowing stars on the upper right
or the green-black spike
thrusting up from the lower left
to blot out village, pinwheels, and all.

# Swan Song

Although I have to say
it's helped my self-esteem,
this feathery white display,
this S-hook's milky gleam,

And yes, of course I enjoy
being part of my very own club
of dudes who towards ducklings deploy
their own hissing brand of snub,

Still, I can't help feeling at times
that this plumage is just a suit,
which unzipped would leave me begrimed,
still scraggly and brown at root,

And although I sail proud in the daylight
cutting through reeds with the best,
those tauntings and quacks of old spite
echo through nights of unrest.

# Mourning Dove

Bodiless sound wafers wobble through sliding doors
the trees ask Who? Who? Who? against the glass
grace for every ear from a hidden source
a string of frisbees flung across a mountain pass

The trees ask Who? Who? Who? against the glass
their queries float invisible above the lawns
a string of frisbees flung across a mountain pass
the thin host flavored with a thousand dawns

Their queries float invisible above the lawns
we take their soft gray tones in with the air
the thin host flavored with a thousand dawns
gentleness spreading lotion for all to share

We take their soft gray tones in with the air
receive them standing, sitting, lying where we are
gentleness spreading lotion for all to share
balm for every skin from an unseen jar

Receive them standing, sitting, lying where we are
bodiless sound wafers wobble through sliding doors
balm for every skin from an unseen jar
grace for every ear from a hidden source

# Sparrow Consciousness

Lunchtime: spinach salad
at the wrought iron table,
feta cheese, tomatoes,
as, to feed the chirping brain,
my eyes lift windoward
from plate and fork
to see what they can see.
There is but one locus of activity:
the seed-filled plastic tube hanging,
its alternating perches
now occupied, now vacant,
vertical way station,
setting for Cirque du Soleil.

Today no gaudy cardinals come to rest,
no costumed blue jays.
Only the intricate choreography of sparrows,
fluttering acrobats in severe brown tights,
forming patterns to a Bach fugue—
the first number on the program,
when neurons are freshest
for attending to pure counterpoint.

To begin, on middle perches, two opposing birds—
heads bobbing
      in and
      out of holes
      by turns—

carved figures on a chiming clock.
A third soars in, stage right—then a fourth—to settle
      top
      and
      bottom.

Sparrow three moves down,
then up again.
Sparrow one, meanwhile, exits over the brown back fence

Two more fly in—then, from around the house, another
chases whichever (???) sparrow
                down, whomever (???) sparrow away
More arrive now, and more—
the mind soon loses track,
needing the birds to be painted
different colors, perhaps,
or an instant replay,
with fluorescent green lines
trailing their movements,
crisscrossed upwards
like laces on an ice skate.

Suddenly, from the clump of fluttering bodies,
a single bird
extricates itself,
hovers perchless and flapping in the air—
        gives up—                then sails off into the trees,

missing a blank bar.

Two more enter,
and for a moment,
all perches are filled,
seeds raining down
into the green dishpan.

I turn my head and all are vacant,
the body after the soul has fled—

feeder still gently rocking.

# Blossoms

Now the town is all over blossoms
breaking out like a teenage face.
Poison for Ira, sweetness for me.
I could write a sonnet every afternoon,
if my sixty-plus Mays hadn't taught me
not to overtry for ecstasy
but pass by the miracle trees
as if they happened every day.

Knowing that on any given day
a particularly voluminous lilac bush
may invite me to reach up
and draw one cluster of purple stars
down towards my nose
and send whole clouds of scent
wafting up into my amygdala,
that tiny almond in the brain
where emotional castles live,
transporting me back
to my grandmother's garden
fifty years ago.

Lately, scientists have begun describing our universe
as almost certainly teeming with life.
And I wonder if on some distant planet
the lilacs bloom year round
and, if so, do the people there
pass by the blossoms as we pass by
ordinary leaves?

Or do they pause, as I do now,
to inhale, reflect,
and relive?

## Waterline

Forget the basin's covering of stretched blue silk.
Ignore the foliage on distant shores
and pay attention only
to the water's undulating edge.
Appreciate the absence of tides.
Follow each nuance of lapping with your ears
until your breath grows soft
and your fists unfold.

Choose a wrinkle
and watch it travel along the selvage
from left to right,
flattened into wet sand by invisible thumbs,
or study a white pebble mildly tumbling
under wavelet after wavelet.

Sit still and memorize
the dance steps of a sandpiper
shifting from leg to leg, oblivious
to miniature breakers,
butterfly effects
of distant motorboats.

Sip the lake's gentleness like steaming tea
and recollect it lovingly
each time you smooth a pillow
or close a door
or intervene
and when you're sitting alone in a room,
remember always

how mottled octagons turn to gold
when the sun comes out from under a cloud.

# What?

After moonlight glazes your favorite lake,
After your infant nestles into your neck,
After trees transmute from green to red and gold,
After words spring unbidden into your idling brain,
After other-worldly soprano notes lift you out of your body,
After laughter shakes your house from cellar to attic,
After long-winded novels on rainy afternoons,
After wonderful news in your mailbox,
After wood floors under your naked soles,
After cocoa and cinnamon toast,
After the peace of a job well done,
And after you learn, finally,
that someone you love
loves you back,

What could any brand of heaven offer
that you would even want?

# Like Water, Like

Flows in dotted lines silver-gray from the showerhead
flows along buzzing wires to the reading lamp
flows out of the stadium around the kiosks and together again
flows from the spigot into the brimming mug
flows past the Adam's apple to the yellow arc
flows along the curbside mixed with dry leaves
flows out into the open sea

Flows through the green lights and under the overpass
flows from the in-box into the mailbox
flows from the rectangle at the top to the circle past the arrow
flows from the paycheck into the jingling drawer
flows from the poet's brain to the waiting page
flows from the trumpet to the clarinet to the violin
flows out into the open sea

Flows from the spewing crater to the museum case
flows from the sun's core to the browning skin
flows from the north pole to the south pole
flows from the uterus to the white gauze
flows from the revolution to the last day
flows to the place beyond flow
flows out into the open sea

# Unclenching

The snow decides
when it will snow,
testing at first
with a flake or three
before making up its mind
in a swirl.
The snow decides—
not some eighth grader
fixed on school closings
willing white moths
out of the blank air.

The hand decides
what bills to sign;
the other mouth can choose
to kiss or not to kiss;
the dog controls his bark,
the moon the moon.
Those boots that come marching
over the ridge will march:
the best we can do
is oppose them.

Dear one, open your hand.
Surrender boots to boots,
kiss to kiss,
snow to snow.
Give back all things
unto themselves
and sleep.

# Acknowledgments

Many thanks to the editors of the following publications, where some of the poems in this book previously appeared:
*Aries:* "Waterline"
*Barbaric Yawp:* "Starry Night" and "Sparrow Consciousness"
*The Chaffin Journal:* "Day after Day"
*Connecticut River Review:* "Holy Week at Work"
*Illuminations:* "The Good Day" and "Just in Case, Darling"
*Plainsong:* "Walking Chelsea after the Sudden Death of a Friend"

Thanks also to Marilyn Churchill, Kathy Edgren, Mary Koral, Chris Lord, Sue Budin and other members of our Sunday morning writing group in Ann Arbor; Ian Fulcher; Anne-Marie Oomen; Richard Tillinghast, Thomas Lynch, and other faculty and students at the Bear River Writer's Conference for feedback and suggestions on my poems. Special thanks to Bruce Bennett, who taught my first creative writing class at Oberlin College in 1969 and came full circle to act as a wonderful poetry mentor, editor, and friend in the 2020s. Thanks to the staff at Finishing Line Press for their excellent work in producing this book. And, of course, thanks to my husband, Ira Glovinsky, for his wisdom, support, and just being Ira.

**Cindy Glovinsky** was born in Des Moines, Iowa in 1948. She attended Des Moines Public Schools and spent her junior and senior years as a violin major at the Interlochen Arts Academy, Interlochen Michigan, about which she published a memoir, *Music, Lakes & Blue Corduroy*. She received a B.A. in English from Oberlin College, after which she moved to Ann Arbor, Michigan, where she has lived ever since.

Having spent most of her adult life in a university town earning further degrees in music, English, and social work, Cindy describes herself as a "professional student" who also held various "day jobs" doing office work at the University of Michigan. She has worked as a clerk-typist, research secretary, administrative assistant, academic editor, clinical social worker, adjunct English instructor, professional organizer, and professional violinist. At present, Cindy is a full-time writer who also enjoys playing the piano.

Cindy currently lives in Ann Arbor with her psychologist husband, Ira Glovinsky and their two cats, Chloe and Sidney. She has one son, Matthew Ferguson, who lives with his family in Lansing and works for the State of Michigan and a stepdaughter, Marni Glovinsky, who lives with her husband in Ann Arbor.

In connection with her work as a professional organizer, Cindy published three self-help books with St. Martin's Press—*Making Peace with the Things in Your Life, One Thing at a Time, and Making Peace with Your Office Life*—and her poetry and creative prose have appeared in various literary magazines, including *Ploughshares, Illuminations, Connecticut River Review, Bear River Review, Pacific Coast Journal, Aries, The Chaffin Journal, Plainsong,* and *Barbaric Yawp. Unclenching* is her first published book of poetry.

www.ingramcontent.com/pod-product-compliance
Lightning Source LLC
Chambersburg PA
CBHW020340170426
43200CB00006B/446